MIDLOTHIAN PUBLIC LIBRARY

3 1614 00199 5407

W9-BIJ-568

E
599.665
KLU

spot

AFRICAN ANIMALS

ZEBRAS

MIDLOTHIAN PUBLIC LIBRARY
14701 S. KENTON AVENUE
MIDLOTHIAN, IL 60445

by Mary Ellen Klukow

AMICUS | AMICUS INK

stripes

teeth

Look for these
words and pictures
as you read.

ears

hoof

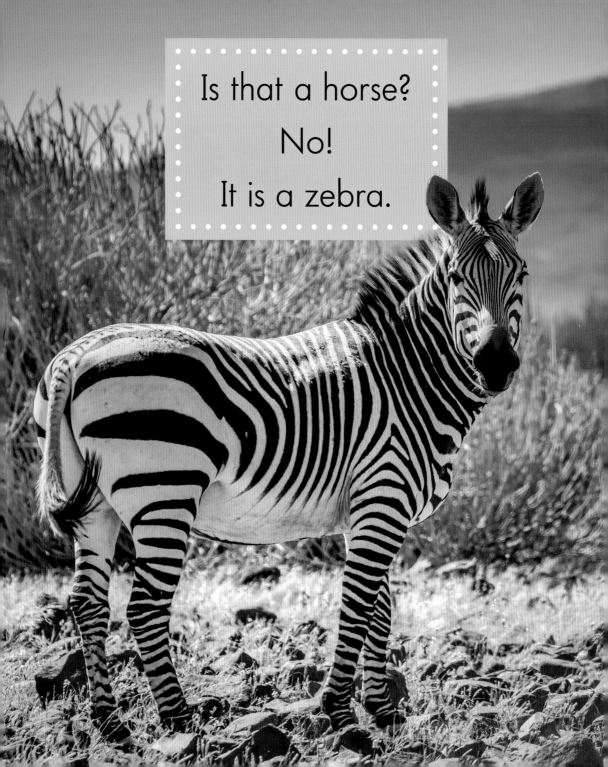

Is that a horse?

No!

It is a zebra.

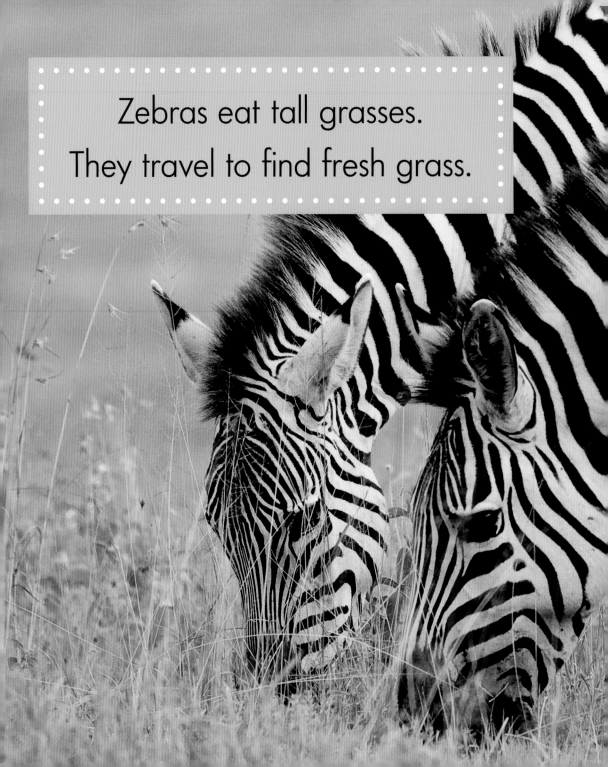

Zebras eat tall grasses.
They travel to find fresh grass.

Look at the stripes.
Baby zebras have brown stripes.
They turn black after one year.

stripes

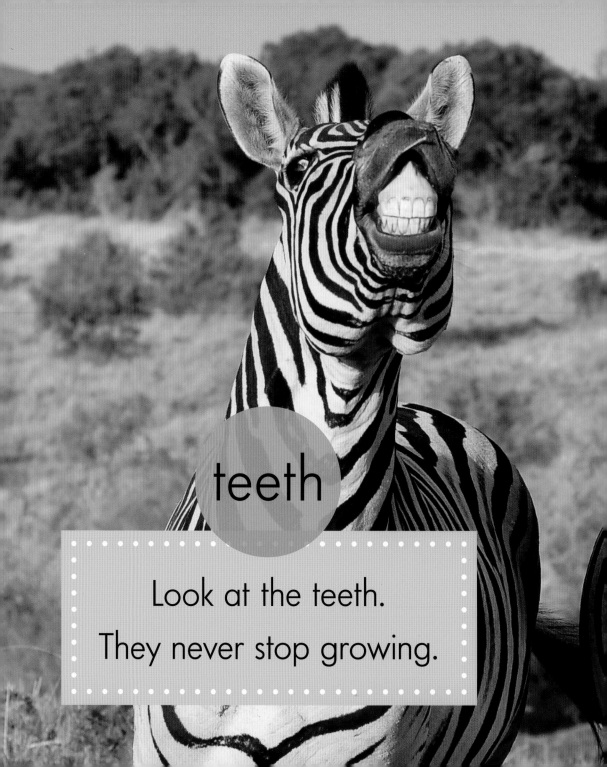

teeth

Look at the teeth.
They never stop growing.

ears

Look at the ears.

Zebras can hear better than you can.

They listen for enemies.

hoof

Look at the hoof.

It is hard.

Zebras kick enemies.

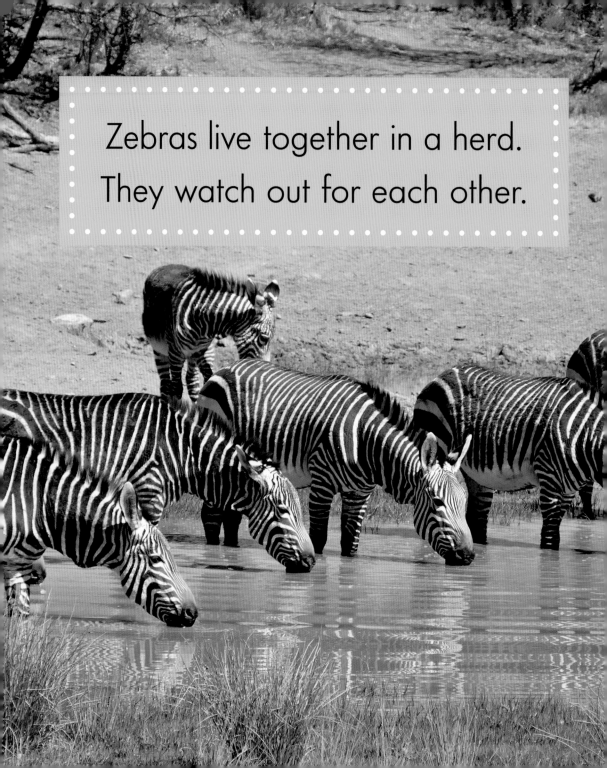

Zebras live together in a herd.
They watch out for each other.

Look at the stripes.
Baby zebras have brown stripes.
They turn black after one year.

stripes

teeth

Look at the teeth.
They never stop growing.

stripes

teeth

Did you find?

ears

Look at the ears.
Zebras can hear better than you can.
They listen for enemies.

ears

hoof

hoof

Look at the hoof.
It is hard.
Zebras kick enemies.

spot

Spot is published by Amicus and Amicus Ink
P.O. Box 1329, Mankato, MN 56002
www.amicuspublishing.us

Copyright © 2020 Amicus.
International copyright reserved in all countries.
No part of this book may be reproduced in any form
without written permission from the publisher.

Library of Congress Cataloging-in-Publication Data
Names: Klukow, Mary Ellen, author.
Title: Zebras / by Mary Ellen Klukow.
Description: Mankato, Minnesota : Amicus, [2020] | Series:
   Spot. African animals | Audience: K to Grade 3. |
Identifiers: LCCN 2018026910 (print) | LCCN 2018031229
   (ebook) | ISBN 9781681517254 (pdf) | ISBN
   9781681516431 (library binding) | ISBN 9781681524290
   (paperback) | ISBN 9781681517254 (ebook)
Subjects: LCSH: Zebras--Africa--Juvenile literature.
Classification: LCC QL737.U62 (ebook) | LCC QL737.U62
   K58 2020 (print) | DDC 599.665/7--dc23
LC record available at https://lccn.loc.gov/2018026910

Printed in China

HC 10 9 8 7 6 5 4 3 2 1
PB 10 9 8 7 6 5 4 3 2 1

Wendy Dieker and Alissa Thielges, editors
Deb Miner, series designer
Ciara Beitlich, book designer
Holly Young, photo researcher

Photos by Shutterstock/Volodymyr
Burdiak Cover; Shutterstock/Anan
Kaewkhammul 1; iStock/Leamus 3;
iStock/jocrebbin 4–5; Shutterstock/
Sheila Fitzgerald 6–7; Shutterstock/
Michael Potter11 8–9; iStock/bazilfoto
10–11; Getty/Paul Souders 12–13;
WikiCommons/Bernard DUPONT 14

ZEBRAS